Butterfly Kisses

BUTTERFLY KISSES

quotes for daily motivation
and renewal

Elley-Ray

SR A NEW MOON BOOK

NEW MOON

is an imprint of Salt River Publishing
Phoenix, Arizona
SaltRiverPublishing.com

First edition
17 16 15   3 2 1   III II I
ISBN 978-0-9893349-8-3

Artwork for cover and flipbook by Jarrod Elvin (see
Colophon)

All Salt River books are available at
SaltRiverPublishing.com/estore/

For Shirley Ellen Doreen Snowe

My darling mother and inspired best friend
shared a number of gentle gifts with me before quietly slipping into a coma and travelling
away. One in particular has lit many a dark
day since her passing.

When I asked, "How will I know if you
are with me after you die?", she simply replied
with a smile, "Look for butterflies". Oh and
the way her blue eyes would dance with a
wisdom of time…

It was a cold April morning 2010, the day
after her death. I fell outside into my empty
garden to find respite and swallow bitter coffee and abundant tears amidst grey skies. The
wind danced and suddenly to my amazement

a beautiful white butterfly flew over the hedge and landed on the bush directly beside me, gently fanning its wings.

That is the magic we must believe in.

I see butterflies everywhere now, on t-shirts, signs, cards, tattoos, flying gaily about – in fact two monarchs landed on my hand this year. Love is constantly with us and we need to give that love to ourselves and those around us. Spirit is eternal. Look for butterflies!

If you flip the pages of *Butterfly Kisses*, you'll see a butterfly emerging there, too.

I offer you this little gift – 365 days of butterfly kisses. **Transform**!

365 quotes

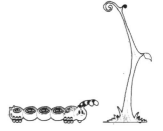

for daily

motivation

and renewal

1

Journey today to the centre
of your creativity to find
multi-verses of twinkling memories.

Yet after brick and steel and stone
are gone, and flesh and blood are
dust, the dream lives on.
ANDERSON M. SCRUGGS

2

Release negativity.

It is cynicism and fear that
freeze life, it is faith that thaws
it out, releases it, sets it free.
HARRY EMERSON FOSDICK

3

Live each day as if it were your last.

So sad, so strange, the days that are no more.

ALFRED TENNYSON

4

See **everything** as an opportunity.

*Small opportunities are often the
beginning of great enterprises.*

DEMOSTHENES

5

Write a poem to yourself.

We can read poetry and recite poetry, but
to live poetry is the symphony of life.

S. Frances Foote

6

May your words come
from a loving heart.

The only way to speak the
truth is to speak lovingly.

Henry David Thoreau

7

Stop finding fault.

Don't look for flaws as you go through life,
And even when you find them,
It is wise and kind to be somewhat blind
And look for the virtue behind them.

ELLA WHEELER WILCOX

8

Delight in your wondrous life.

Life is the childhood of our immortality.

GOETHE

9

Take the emphasis off yourself.

If you want to be miserable, think about yourself, about what you want, what you like, what respect people ought to pay you, and what people think of you.

CHARLES KINGSLEY

10

Be patient.

Genius is eternal patience.

MICHELANGELO

11

Honesty is the key.

*Truth…is the highest summit
of art and of life.*

HENRY FREDERIC DANIEL

12

Create new ideas for yourself.

*Greater than any army with banners
is an idea whose time has come.*

VICTOR HUGO

13

Go to the symphony.

Where words fail, music speaks.

HANS CHRISTIAN ANDERSON

14

Slow down!

*There is more to life
than increasing its speed.*

MAHATMA GANDHI

15

Be a loyal friend.
Find time and listen.

*To be trusted is a greater
compliment than to be loved.*

GEORGE MACDONALD

16

Give thanks today.

*There is not a more pleasing exercise
of the mind than gratitude.*

JOSEPH ADDISON

17

Consider how you can
become a wise being.

The days that make us happy make us wise.

JOHN MASEFIELD

18

Never lose hope.

*Everything that is done in the
world is done by hope.*

MARTIN LUTHER

19

Live in the moment.

*Be not anxious about tomorrow. Do today's
duty, fight today's temptation, and do not
weaken and distract yourself by looking
forward to things you cannot see, and
could not understand if you saw them.*

UNKNOWN

20

Be content.

*When we cannot find contentment in
ourselves, it is useless to seek it elsewhere.*

FRANÇOIS DE LA ROCHEFOUCAULD

21

Sit in solitude.

*I love to be alone. I never found
the companion that was so
companionable as solitude.*

HENRY DAVID THOREAU

22

Strengthen your courage.

*He that loses wealth loses mud;
But he that loses courage loses all.*

CERVANTES

23

Make an effort.

*It is hard to fail, but it is worse never
to have tried to succeed. In this life
we get nothing save by effort.*

THEODORE ROOSEVELT

24

Find the courage within you
to go after your dreams.

*Hope awakens courage. He who
can implant courage in the human
soul is the best physician.*

VON KNEBEL

25

Release envy from your life.

*With a few flowers in my garden,
half a dozen pictures and some
books, I live without envy.*

Lope De Vega

26

Do a favour for someone today.

*What do we live for, if it is not to make
life less difficult to each other?*

George Eliot

27

Go **big** or go home.

*Do not let the good things of life
rob you of the best things.*

Maltbie D. Babcock

28

Use a happy face or heart
icon on messages.

*We are all of us fellow-passengers on the
same planet and we are all of us equally
responsible for the happiness and the
well-being of the world in
which we happen to live.*

Hendrick Willem Van Loon

29

Use your brain today.

I think, therefore I am.

RENÉ DESCARTES

30

Fail at something today and learn.

*Probably he who never made a
mistake never made a discovery.*

SMILES

31

Think like a dog today and be loyal.

*An ounce of loyalty is worth
a pound of cleverness.*

UNKNOWN

32

Close your eyes and
make a wish today.

*It seems to me we can never give up
longing and wishing while we are
thoroughly alive. There are certain
things we feel to be beautiful and good
and we must hunger after them.*

GEORGE ELIOT

33

Write, paint, dance, perform, create.

Art is more Godlike than science.
Science discovers; art creates.
JOHN OPIE

34

Stay the course.

There is genius and power in persistence.
It conquers all opposers; it gives
confidence; it annihilates obstacles."
ORISON SWEET MARDEN

35

What are your merits?

*Charms strike the sight, but
merit wins the soul.*

ALEXANDER POPE

36

Support a humanitarian
cause today.

*The joys and sorrows of others are
ours as much as theirs, and in proper
time as we feel this and learn to live
so that the whole world shares the life
that flows through us, do our minds
learn the secret of Peace.*

UNKNOWN

37

The Good, the Bad, the Ugly –
which would you choose?

*Goodness is the only investment
that never fails.*

HENRY DAVID THOREAU

38

Keep looking forward!

*When the past calls, let it go to voicemail.
Believe me, it has nothing new to say.*

UNKNOWN

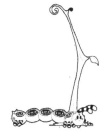

39

Write out your dreams today.

*Go confidently in the direction of your
dreams! Live the life you've imagined!*

Henry David Thoreau

40

Have utter faith in yourself.

*Faith is to believe what we do not
see, and the reward of this faith
is to see what we believe.*

St. Augustine

41

Take fear out of the equation.

*You gain strength, courage and confidence
by every experience in which you
really stop to look fear in the face.*

ELEANOR ROOSEVELT

42

Trust yourself to make
the right decisions.

*Self-distrust is the cause of
most of our failures.*

BOVEE

43

See the beauty in life.

If the day and the night are such that
you greet them with joy, and life emits a
fragrance like flowers and sweet-scented
herbs, is more elastic, more starry, more
immortal — that is your success.

HENRY DAVID THOREAU

44

Be honest with yourself.

This above all: to thine own self be true,
And it must follow, as the night the day,
Thou canst not then be false
to any man.

SHAKESPEARE

45

Avoid taking advantage of people.

*We too often love things and use people when
we should be using things and loving people.*

Reuel Howe

46

Children laugh 400 times
a day and we laugh 12
to 15. Laugh more.

*Laughing is the sensation of feeling good all
over, and showing it principally in one spot.*

Josh Billings

47

Fully open and receive
love from others today.

All you need is love…
THE BEATLES

48

Spread and share your divine
light with others. Remember,
a single candle can light
another and multiply.

*Let your constant aim be to being a bit of
sunshine into the life of every being you meet.*
UNKNOWN

49

Forgive.

Love the truth but pardon the error.

VOLTAIRE

50

Run through a sprinkler
today and get soaked.

*A great man is he who has not
lost the heart of a child.*

MENCIUS

51

Everything you need is right here.

Use well the moment. What the hour brings for your use is in your power. And what you can best understand is just the thing that lies nearest to your hand.

GOETHE

52

Be a disciple disciplined
in the Art of Living.

*The only way to do great work is to love what you do. If you haven't found it yet, keep looking.
Don't settle.*

STEVE JOBS

53

Make a wish when you see 11:11 on
a clock, receipt or license plate.

*Life is like photography. You need
the negatives to develop.*

Unknown

54

Turn every negative into a positive.

*I am thankful for all those who said No to
me. It's because of them I'm doing it myself.*

Albert Einstein

55

Be your own visionary with
gems of infinite worth.

*Forget all the reasons it won't work and
believe the one reason that it will.*

Unknown

56

Get out of your head
and into your heart.

*Don't be afraid to stand for what you
believe in, even if it means standing alone.*

Unknown

57

Create a mission for yourself today,
to make the world a better place.

*You make the world a better place by
making yourself a better person.*

Scott Sorell

58

See the big picture.

*Build your own dreams or someone
else will hire you to build theirs.*

Farrah Gray

59

You are a divine creation.
Expect miracles!

*Being happy doesn't mean that everything
is perfect. It means that you've decided
to look beyond the imperfections.*

UNKNOWN

60

Write an inspiration and pass it on.

*Life is short, live it. Love is rare, grab it.
Anger is bad, dump it. Fear is awful, face
it. Remembering is sweet, cherish it.*

UNKNOWN

61

You don't need to fix your
whole life all at once.

*Life has two rules: #1 Never quit
#2 Always remember rule #1.*

<small>Unknown</small>

62

Be careful.

*Three things you cannot recover in life:
The **word** after it's said, the **moment**
after it's missed and **time** after it's gone.*

<small>Unknown</small>

63

Go for a long walk and
see what nature sends you
as a message or gift.

*You will succeed best when you put
the restless, anxious side of affairs
out of mind, and allow the restful
side to live in your thoughts.*

MARGARET STOWE

64

Never doubt yourself.

Nothing is impossible to a valiant heart.

UNKNOWN

65

You deserve all things
great and beautiful.

*My life is evolutionary and revolutionary.
My attitude of openness, expectation and
observation yields me a sense of abundance.*

JULIA CAMERON

66

How can you make the world
a better place today? Choose
an action and do it!

*Love and desire are the spirits'
wings to great deeds.*

GOETHE

67

What are you grateful for today? Give thanks.

Gratitude is the fairest blossom which springs from the soul.

BALLOCE

68

What doors are you willing to open today?

Go to your bosom; knock there, and ask your heart what it doth know…

SHAKESPEARE

69

Spread your wings and fly.

To understand the heights we can reach, we must first be willing to jump from the nest.

UNKNOWN

70

Have absolute faith in your talent.

I would like to be remembered as someone who did the best she could with the talent she had.

JK ROWLING

71

Volunteer your time at a soup kitchen, old folks' home, children's hospital.

It is a denial of justice not to stretch out a helping hand to the fallen. That is the common right of humanity.

SENECA

72

Write a love letter to yourself.

What cannot letters inspire? They have souls; they can speak; they have in them all that force which expresses the transports of the heart…

HÉLOÏSE TO ABELARD

73

Share with those less fortunate.

*Give with open hands and a
heart that is even more open.*

UNKNOWN

74

Praise yourself.

*The more you praise and celebrate your
life, the more there is in life to celebrate.*

OPRAH WINFREY

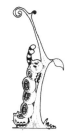

75

Put a jade plant in the back left hand corner of your house to attract Feng Shui abundance.

Abundance is not something we acquire. It is something we tune into.
WAYNE DYER

76

Make an effort to greet and speak to at least three people you don't know today.

Smile at strangers and you just might change a life.
STEVE MARABOLI

77

Know that you are not perfect and mistakes are opportunities to **grow**.

"We learn from failure, not from success!
BRAM STOKER

78

Watch the sunrise. Set your alarm and experience the magic!

Watching the clock is not the same as watching a sunrise.
SOPHIA BEFFORD PIERCE

79

Sing out loud today.

*Music washes away from the
soul the dust of everyday life.*

RED AUERBACH

80

Start a four-week meditation
"Manifest Your Destiny" by
Kelly Howell (on youtube) to
strengthen your resolve.

*Determination gives you the
resolve to keep going in spite of the
roadblocks that lie before you.*

DENIS WAITLEY

81

Create a **vision board** at home
with words, images, inspirations,
dreams. Be specific and include
all the gifts you wish to experience
in your life. Sign the back of it.

*Envisioning the end is enough
to put the means in motion.*
DORTHEA BRANDE

82

All you have to do today is **believe**!

*Most people are living lives
of quiet desperation.*
HENRY DAVID THOREAU

83

When walking outside today,
look **up** to the eternal sky rather
than down to the ground.

*Blue skies smiling at me. Nothing
but blue skies do I see.*

IRVING BERLIN

84

Take action. What
you-nique essence is calling to
be expressed through you?

*Don't compare yourself with
anyone in this world... If you do
so, you are insulting yourself.*

BILL GATES

85

Write with your opposite hand
today to strengthen another
part of your glorious brain.

*The brain is like a muscle. When it is in use
we feel very good. Understanding is joyous.*

CARL SAGAN

86

What is blooming in your
creative garden today? Water and
nurture this blossoming growth.

*The worst enemy to
creativity is self-doubt.*

SYLVIA PLATH

87

Don't procrastinate, accomplish
a major task in forwarding
your dreams today.

*Only put off until tomorrow what you
are willing to die having left undone.*

PABLO PICASSO

88

Write a note to yourself to
manifest a dream today.

*If you have a dream, keep it. But
write it down and take appropriate
actions to see it manifest.*

TF HODGE

89

What you feed will grow
bigger. So feed joy and hope,
not fear and despair.

Hope is the thing with feathers
That perches in the soul
And sings the tune without the words
And never stops at all.

EMILY DICKINSON

90

Find yourself, don't hide
behind your baggage.

Knowing yourself is the
beginning of all wisdom.

ARISTOTLE

91

Drink more water.

Water does not resist. Water flows. When you plunge your hand into it, all you feel is a caress. Water is not a solid wall, it will not stop you. But water always goes where it wants to go, and nothing in the end can stand against it. Water is patient. Dripping water wears away a stone. Remember that, my child. Remember you are half water. If you can't go through an obstacle, go around it. Water does.

MARGARET ATWOOD

92

Light a green candle and manifest abundant love.

Look at how a single candle can both defy and define the darkness.

ANNE FRANK

93

Donate money to your favourite charity.

There is no exercise better for the heart than reaching down and lifting people up.

JOHN HOLMES

94

Have peace in your heart and
know you are exactly where
you are supposed to be.

*The wise man looks inside his
heart and finds eternal peace.*

HINDU PROVERB

95

Trust yourself to know.

*None of us knows what might happen even
the next minute, yet still we go forward.
Because we trust. Because we have Faith.*

PAULO COELHO

96

Power up your internal
creative battery, sit in silence
in stillness and nature.

*Climb the mountains and get their good
tidings. Nature's peace will flow into you as
sunshine flows into trees. The winds will
blow their own freshness into you, and the
storms their energy, while cares will drop
away from you like the leaves of Autumn.*

JOHN MUIR

97

Envision yourself as a glorious
rainbow, in full spectrum waves,
streaming bright colours.

*Dare to love yourself as if you were
a rainbow with gold at both ends.*

ABERJHANI

98

Receive vision and guidance,
find a mentor or teacher.

*The true tragedy in most people's lives is
that they are far better than they imagine
themselves to be and, as a result, end up
being much less than they might be.*

EARL R. SMITH II

99

Be dedicated, disciplined and determined. Have a plan.

True freedom is impossible without a mind made free by discipline.

MORTIMER J. ADLER

100

Feed the birds.

The bird dares to break the shell, then the shell breaks open and the bird can fly openly. This is the simplest principle of success. You dream, you dare and you fly.

ISRAELMORE AYIVOR

101

Exercise. Take a yoga class.
Walk the dog. **Move** your body!

Consciousness is only possible
through change; change is only
possible through movement.
ALDOUS HUXLEY

102

Get eight hours of rest nightly.
Restorative sleep keeps us strong.

Each night, when I go to sleep, I
die. And the next morning, when
I wake up, I am reborn.
MAHATMA GANDHI

103

Be the captain of your own career.
Only you can steer your ship.

*The compass rose is nothing but
a star with an infinite number of
rays pointing in all directions.*

Vera Nazarain

104

The early bird gets the worm.
Attack each day with a
lust for creation.

Just Do It

Nike logo

105

Tell someone you love them today.

*You know you're in love when you
can't fall asleep because reality is
finally better than your dreams.*

Dr. Seuss

106

Do something that terrifies you.
Fear is just **joy** without the breath.

*You must do the thing you
think you cannot do.*

Eleanor Roosevelt

107

Fly a kite.

Life is not life at all without delight.

Coventry Patmore

108

Remove wheat and gluten from your diet and see how you feel.

*I am a better person when
I have less on my plate.*

Elizabeth Gilbert

109

Be grateful for your sight. See!

Unity is vision; it must have been part of the process of learning to see.

HENRY ADAMS

110

Take a teaspoon of apple cider vinegar every day to neutralize the acid in your body.

A fit, healthy body – that is the best fashion statement.

JESS C. SCOTT

111

Add colour to your office
and a whoopee cushion.

The purest and most thoughtful minds
are those which love colour the most.

JOHN RUSKIN

112

Awaken your unique
and authentic voice.

We have to dare to be ourselves,
however frightening or strange
that self may prove to be.

MAY SARTON

113

Bake cookies for your neighbours.

*Cookies were much better eaten than
sold, and they were best homemade.*

JESSE HAUBERT

114

Surrender yourself, tune
into the divine light… Open,
open, open your heart.

*If I were to take down the walls to let
your love in, I would not only free my
heart, I'd free the world. There shall be no
barrier for love to be contained. A heart
with a pulse in rhythm connects us all.*

JASON MICHAEL RATLIFF

115

Celebrate.

*If you don't feel it, flee from it. Go where
you are celebrated, not merely tolerated.*

PAUL F. DAVIS

116

Today…create new pathways, new
structures, new foundations and
new imaginings for a new story.

*If you want something new, you have
to stop doing something old.*

PETER F. DUCKER

117

Look at this day and be
grateful for **all** that you are.

*Let us be grateful to the people who
make us happy; they are the charming
gardeners who make our souls blossom.*

Marcel Proust

118

Release negative feelings
that weigh upon you.

*When you succumb to cynicism, darkness,
pessimism and sarcasm you are
amplifying imbalance and negativity.*

Bryant McGill

119

Give the gift of You echoing and transforming then to Now.

When she transformed into a butterfly, the caterpillars spoke not of her beauty, but of her weirdness. They wanted her to change back into what she always had been. But she had wings.

DEAN JACKSON

120

Tell a joke.

A loyal friend laughs at your jokes when they're not so good, and sympathizes with your problems when they're not so bad.

ARNOLD H. GLASGOW

121

Volunteer to walk dogs at
your local animal shelter.

*Remember that the happiest people are not
those getting more, but those giving more.*

H. JACKSON BROWN JR.

122

Use your voice to minister help
and support to the world.

*The voice of beauty speaks softly; it creeps
only into the most fully awakened souls.*

FRIEDRICH NIETZSCHE

123

Read a book to a child.

If you want your children to be intelligent, read them fairy tales. If you want them to be more intelligent, read them more fairy tales.

ALBERT EINSTEIN

124

Believe in magic!

The moment you doubt whether you can fly, you cease forever to be able to do it.

JM BARRIE

125

Mentor someone new.
Pay it forward.

*You don't need much to change the
entire world for the better. You can start
with the most ordinary ingredients. You
can start with the world you've got.*

CATHERINE RYAN HYDE

126

Send your sweetheart a
postcard even when you are
not away on vacation.

*The world before us is a postcard, and I
imagine the story we are writing on it.*

MARY E. PEARSON

127

Speak in an accent from a foreign country and see if you can convince people.

I worked the drive-through at McDonald's and tried out different accents – Italian, Russian, Irish.
JAMES FRANCO

128

Read a book.

I have always imagined that paradise will be a kind of library.
JORGE LUIS BORGES

129

Pray for someone else to thrive.

Prayer is not an old woman's idle amusement.
Properly understood and applied, it is
the most potent instrument of action.
MAHATMA GANDHI

130

Play a board game that
challenges your mind.

Life has but one true charm: the
charm of the game. But what if we're
indifferent to whether we win or lose?
CHARLES BAUDELAIRE

131

Clean your windows, literally
and metaphorically.

*The window to the universe
opens inward and outward.*

Daniel Lee Edstrom

132

Leave your ego at the door.

*You never really learn much from
hearing yourself speak.*

George Clooney

133

Live your dreams.

Preparing to live your dream is postponing it. You are either living it, or not.

ALAN COHEN

134

Dissolve, cleanse and transform fear.

Tell your heart that the fear of suffering is worse than the suffering itself. And that no heart has ever suffered when it goes in search of its dreams, because every second of the search is a second's encounter with God and with eternity.

PAULO COELHO

135

Drive a Go Cart or Paddleboat.

*Each new day is another chapter in the
unfolding promise of deliverance and life.*

ELIZABETH GEORGE

136

Imagine yourself as a hug(e)
powerful, amazing gift to the world.

*May it be a light to you in dark
places, when all other lights go out.*

JRR TOLKIEN

137

Know you are a doorway between
the present and past and future.
Make sure you are not closed
to the infinite possibilities.

*Sometimes you don't know when
you're taking the first step through a
door until you're already inside.*
ANN VOSKAMP

138

For today, how are we fulfilling
love's desire to be shared?

*Love is that condition in which the happiness
of another person is essential to your own.*
ROBERT A. HEINLEIN

139

Turn your mattress over
and flip it upside down.

I keep odd hours.
I keep them stuffed under my mattress.

JAROD KINTZ

140

How do you honour yourself?

There is nothing so rewarding
as to make people realize
that they are worthwhile
in this world.

BOB ANDERSON

Put an EMF magnet on your computer to reduce the energy it emits (while you're at it, do the fridge, microwave, cell phone, etc). Try Bio Pro magnets.

We, and the universe we live in, produce and operate in a sea of natural and unnatural electrical and magnetic fields. Our bodies are really electromagnetic machines. We can't move a muscle or produce a thought without an electrical impulse and wherever there is electricity, a magnetic field is also produced, which is why we link the two together into one word: electromagnetic.

ANN LOUISE GITTLEMAN

142

Look in the mirror and say
"Today I give all of me to the
world with joy and love."

*Because you're a creation of God,
you reflect the divine qualities of
creativity, wisdom and love.*

DOREEN VIRTUE

143

Organize your desktop
and clear out old files.

*A cluttered desk is
a cluttered mind.*

UNKNOWN

144

Put your best foot forward.

It's possible to walk out of your house with 'local' footsteps, printing them one by one till they go on to make 'global' consequences! Go, make a safe journey!

ISRAELMORE AYIVOR

145

Take a 'selfy' of yourself smiling and tweet it.

If you're reading this...
Congratulations, you're alive.
If that's not something to smile about,
then I don't know what is.

CHAD SUGG

When brushing your teeth, make
sure you brush your tongue and
gums as well, to increase circulation
and oral health. Floss, too.

*In the morning I brush my teeth with
hope, and at night before bed I brush
them with defeat. Both are mint flavoured,
so I try not to get them mixed up.*

JAROD KINTZ

147

Do your taxes and keep
your receipts organized.

*To be in hell is to drift; to be
in heaven is to steer.*

GEORGE BERNARD SHAW

148

Listen to the birds singing.

*I pray to the birds because they
remind me of what I love rather than
what I fear. And at the end of my
prayers, they teach me how to listen.*

TERRY TEMPEST WILLIAMS

149

Watch a great movie
and let yourself cry.

*Tears shed for another person are not a sign
of weakness. They are a sign of a pure heart.*

JOSÉ N. HARRIS

150

Wear a silly hat in public.

*The most evident sign of wisdom
is continued cheerfulness.*

MICHEL DE MONTAIGNE

151

Buy yourself a flowering
potted plant.

A flower blossoms for its own joy.
OSCAR WILDE

152

Wake up, another great day
of alive loving is ours.

*Close your eyes and turn your face
into the wind. Feel it sweep along your
skin in an invisible ocean of exultation.
Suddenly, you know you are alive.*
VERA NAZARIAN

153

Stand on one leg while waiting
in line and try to balance.

*Faith gives you an inner strength and a
sense of balance and perspective in life.*
GREGORY PECK

154

Go to the theatre.

*Everything I learned I learned
from the movies.*
AUDREY HEPBURN

155

Remember that you are constantly
dancing at the heart of We.

Dance is the hidden language of the soul.

MARTHA GRAHAM

156

Be generous. What you
give away, you will receive –
the universal flow of energy.

*Because I was more often happy for other
people, I got to spend more time being
happy. And as I saw more light in everybody
else, I seemed to have more myself.*

VICTORIA MORAN

157

Birth a new thought, a new reality,
a new **hope** for our future.

*We dream to give ourselves hope.
To stop dreaming — well, that's like
saying you can never change your fate.*

Amy Tan

158

Breathe in **love**. Breathe out **thanks**.

*This is where it all begins.
Everything starts here, today.*

David Nicholls

159

Update and create a new business
card with a unique brand.

*Logos and branding are so important.
In a big part of the world, people
cannot read French or English — but
are great in remembering signs.*

KARL LAGERFELD

160

Buy sparklers and light up
every single one tonight.

*We shall go wild with fireworks...
And they will plunge into the sky
and shatter the darkness.*

NATSUKI TAKAYA

161

Go swimming and do a
somersault in the water.

The water doesn't know how old you are.

Dara Torres

162

Put an amethyst crystal
in your work space.

May crystals give you power!

Isabel Walbourne

163

Go to your local art
gallery or museum.

*Painting is poetry that is seen rather
than felt, and poetry is painting
that is felt rather than seen.*

LEONARDO DA VINCI

164

Don't wear underpants for one day.

*Creativity can often blossom in
the absence of restrictions.*

ANONYMOUS

165

Find a four-leafed clover.

I'm a great believer in luck, and I find the harder I work the more I have of it.

THOMAS JEFFERSON

166

Buy a magazine subscription of your choice.

In a magazine, one can get — from cover to cover — 15 to 20 different ideas about life and how to live it.

MAYA ANGELOU

167

Open the windows and let the
air blow through your home.

*Another glorious day, the air as delicious
to the lungs as nectar to the tongue.*

JOHN MUIR

168

Go to a sports event and cheer
for the underdog team.

*We have a mission to others – to add to their
cheer. This we cannot do unless we have first
learned the lesson of cheerfulness ourselves.*

J.R. MILLER

169

Wear red on your feet today.

Mars tugs at the human imagination like no other planet. With a force mightier than gravity, it attracts the eye to the shimmering red presence in the clear night sky.

JOHN NOBLE WILFORD

170

Walk by a river, lake or ocean and listen to the moving water.

It is life, I think, to watch the water. We can learn so many things.

NICHOLAS SPARKS

171

Remember, whoever is asking
the questions has control of the
conversation. When asked a
question, respond with a question…

*How old are you? How old
do you want me to be?
Judge a man by his questions
rather than by his answers.*
VOLTAIRE

172

Rearrange your workspace
to create a new view.

A change is as good as a rest.
WINSTON CHURCHILL

173

Gargle with sea salt and water
if your throat feels a tad
sore – keep infection out.

*There must be something strangely sacred
in salt. It is in our tears and in the sea.*

KAHLIL GIBRAN

174

Take a nap during the day.
Churchill lived on less than
4 hours of sleep per night by
taking little naps during the day.

*With great power comes a
great need to take a nap.*

RICK RIORDAN

175

Don't overeat.

You are likely to vomit your dreams if you take too much at a time. Take it one after the other and don't over-eat the dreams you have! Dream big, but start small!

ISRAELMORE AYIVOR

176

Conserve your energy.

If you want to find the secrets of the universe, think in terms of energy, frequency and vibration.

NIKOLA TESLA

177

Stand by your conviction and
have an opinion that you share.

I meant what I said and I said what I meant.
DR. SEUSS

178

Vote!

*Always vote for principle, though
you may vote alone.*
JOHN QUINCY ADAMS

179

Go and watch a 3D animation
movie with the glasses and grab
a big bag of buttered popcorn.

*Animation can explain whatever the
mind of man can conceive. This
facility makes it the most versatile and
explicit means of communication yet
devised for quick mass appreciation.*
WALT DISNEY COMPANY

180

Plant flowers at the grave
of someone you've lost.

I must have flowers, always, and always.
CLAUDE MONET

181

Write out your new year's
resolutions and put them
under your pillow.

Resolve and thou art free.

HENRY WADSWORTH LONGFELLOW

182

Take a hot air balloon ride.

*Being forgiven is like having all the worst
bits of yourself stuffed into a balloon
and then having that balloon set free.*

SHANNON WIERSBITZKY

183

While waiting in traffic,
smile at a stranger.

*When your action is gone, and all that's left
is motionlessness, I'll be there, whistling.*

JAROD KINTZ

184

Write your politician regarding
issues you would like to see
changed. Have a say!

*Why is it that we all say we hate our
hypocritical politicians being controlled
by special interest groups, and every
election we vote them in again.*

COLLEEN HITCHCOCK

185

Have a party for no reason.

*I believe when life gives you lemons,
you should make lemonade — and try
to find someone whose life has given
them vodka, and have a party.*

RON WHITE

186

Do a walking meditation
under a clear blue sky.

*Feelings come and go like clouds in a windy
sky. Conscious breathing is my anchor.*

THÍCH NHẤT HẠNH

187

It is time to vibrate
immortal enlightened
communications forward.

*Enlightenment is man's release from his
self-incurred tutelage. Tutelage is man's
inability to make use of his understanding
without direction from another. Self-
incurred is this tutelage when its cause
lies not in lack of reason but in lack of
resolution and courage to use it without
direction from another. Sapere aude!
'Have courage to use your own reason!' –
that is the motto of enlightenment.*

IMMANUEL KANT

188

Imitate a chicken and really
try to sound like one.

*His mouth formed an O with lips torn angry
in laying duck's eggs from a chicken's rectum.*

NATHANAEL WEST

189

Do a crossword puzzle
or brain teaser.

Why should things be easy to understand?

THOMAS PYNCHON

190

Throw away your frying pan
and buy a new toilet seat.

*The flush toilet, more than any single
invention, has 'civilized' us in a way that
religion and law could never accomplish!*
THOMAS LYNCH

191

Go to a self-help conference
and open up to possibilities.

*I went to a bookstore and asked
the saleswoman, 'Where's the self-
help section?' She said if she told
me, it would defeat the purpose.*
GEORGE CARLIN

192

There is a creative pulse in your heart, calling you to centre. Listen deeply and accept this gift.

Creativity is allowing yourself to make mistakes. Art is knowing which ones to keep.
SCOTT ADAMS

193

Build a sandcastle on a beach and then get buried in the sand.

In every outthrust headland, in every curving beach, in every grain of sand there is the story of the earth.
RACHEL CARSON

194

Be the king or queen
of your domain.

It matters not how strait the gate,
How charged with punishments the scroll,
I am the master of my fate:
I am the captain of my soul.
WILLIAM ERNEST HENLEY

195

Try to fast for one day each week.

Everyone can perform magic, everyone
can reach his goals, if he is able to think,
if he is able to wait, if he is able to fast.
HERMANN HESSE

196

Get your eyes and hearing checked
before you notice a problem.

*A healthy society begins with
healthy individuals.*

SABINA NORE

197

Eat an organic apple each day.

*Before the war an apple tree had
stood behind the church. It was an
apple tree that ate its own apples.*

HERTA MÜLLER

198

Even when a storm is raging,
the sun still shines behind the
clouds. Tune in to the light!

*A pessimist sees the difficulty in every
opportunity; an optimist sees the
opportunity in every difficulty.*

WINSTON CHURCHILL

199

Negativity takes double the energy
of positivity. So be positive!

*It is not what happens to you that matters;
it is how you feel about it that does.*

SHANNON L. ALDER

200

Shake someone's hand today.

*Let your handshake be a greater
bond than any written contract.*

STEVE MARABOLI

201

Fly with eagles.

*If we never had the courage to take
a leap of faith, we'd be cheating God
out of a chance to mount us up with
wings like eagles and watch us soar.*

JEN STEPHENS

202

Risk it all.

Nothing is impossible to a willing heart.

THOMAS HEYWOOD

203

Remind yourself how brilliant you are.

The power of a person's mind is in the strength at the depth of his heart throughout the length of his life.

ANUJ SOMANY

204

Get a full-body massage.

When the body gets working appropriately,
the force of gravity can flow through — then
spontaneously the body heals itself.
IDA ROLF

205

Hold the door open for
people today and always.

Respect for ourselves guides our morals;
respect for others guides our manners.
LAURENCE STERNE

206

Take your best friend to lunch.

*Two people who are true friends are
like two bodies with one soul.*

CHAIM POTOK

207

Install a pure water
system in your home.

*If truth prevails, the contributions of a
courageous physician and a brilliant engineer
to the conquest of waterborne disease will
still be remembered in another hundred years.*

MICHAEL J. McGUIRE

208

There's no time for a Pity
Party. Don't go there.

*I'm a fairly tormented artist, but
I'm less willing to indulge myself in
self-pity, outside of song writing.*

DAVE MATTHEWS

209

Eat organic cinnamon.

*If you build up the soil with organic
material, the plants will do just fine.*

JOHN HARRISON

210

Take proper breaks during your
day and leave the noise behind.

Silence is a source of great strength.

Lao Tzu

211

Spend time with your family:
they should come first.

*Let us make one point, that we meet
each other with a smile when it is difficult
to smile. Smile at each other, make
time for each other in your family.*

Mother Teresa

212

Chew bubblegum and see how big a bubble you can create.

The world as we have created it is a process of our thinking. It cannot be changed without changing our thinking.

ALBERT EINSTEIN

213

Do 20 push ups and 20 burpy jumps every day. Move!

The first time I see a jogger smiling, I'll consider it.

JOAN RIVERS

214

Don't use your cell phone
for one day – lose it.

*Twenty years from now you will be
more disappointed by the things you
didn't do than by the ones you did. So
throw off the bowlines. Sail away from
the safe harbor. Catch the trade winds
in your sails. Explore. Dream.*

MARK TWAIN

215

Make money in your PJs today.

Wake up and be awesome.

UNKNOWN

216

Start up a local softball league.

The nice thing about teamwork is that you always have others on your side.

MARGARET CARTY

217

Pass on practical information with humour.

I don't trust anyone who doesn't laugh.

MAYA ANGELOU

218

Buy an old comic book and read
as the characters – aloud.

It may be true that the only reason the
comic book industry now exists is for this
purpose – to create characters for movies,
board games and other types of merchandise.
ALAN MOORE

219

Run a marathon or cheer
on someone you know.

The happiest people don't necessarily
have the best of everything. They
just make the best of everything.
ANONYMOUS

220

Take the (K)not out of your life.
Have you ever said, "It's not
possible", "It's not in my budget",
"It's not that I don't want to...",
"Not right now"? That (K)not
blocks any positive flow so take
the (K)not out of your vocabulary.

*Dwelling on the negative simply
contributes to its power.*
SHIRLEY MacLAINE

221

Have faith that everything
you desire is possible.

*When spider webs unite, they
can tie up a lion.*

ETHIOPIAN PROVERB

222

Get your teeth cleaned – a
smile is everything.

*Let my soul smile through my heart and
my heart smile through my eyes, that I
may scatter rich smiles in sad hearts.*

PARAMAHANSA YOGANANDA

223

Go on a picnic in the country.

*In everyone's life there's a person
we will never forget... and a
summer where it all started.*

UNKNOWN

224

Live the life you are meant to live.

Be yourself; everyone else is already taken.

OSCAR WILDE

225

Simply **be**.

*I might repeat to myself slowly and
soothingly a list of quotations beautiful
from minds profound – if I can
remember any of the damn things.*

DOROTHY PARKER

226

Look at images of sacred geometry.

*There is geometry in the humming
of the strings, there is music in
the spacing of the spheres.*

PYTHAGORAS

227

Read a newspaper and know
what is topical and current.

*What matters is to live in the present,
live now, for every moment is now. It is
your thoughts and acts of the moment
that create your future. The outline
of your future path already exists, for
you created its pattern by your past.*

SAI BABA

228

Join a choir and sing in unison.

If all of us acted in unison as I act individually there would be no wars and no poverty. I have made myself personally responsible for the fate of every human being who has come my way.

ANAIS NIN

229

Dye your hair a different colour.

As an actor, particularly because I'm — I would call myself a character actor — I change my look, my physical appearance and my body, my hair color, my whatever all the time for a role.

LYNN REDGRAVE

230

Recognize that every word, note, thought, tone and emotion has a geometric, vibrational signature. So do you.

The harmony of the world is made manifest in form and number, and the heart and soul and all the poetry of natural philosophy are embodied in the concept of mathematical beauty.
SIR D'ARCY WENTWORTH THOMPSON

231

Submerge yourself under water,
whether a pool, lake, ocean
or bathtub. Just hold your
breath and be supported.

We are all born of water, and to return to
it imbues us with a sense of genesis.

ANONYMOUS

232

Follow a difficult recipe you have
never cooked before, to the letter
and then add your own special
ingredient not on the recipe.

The true method of knowledge is experiment.

WILLIAM BLAKE

233

Push your potential on
a day-to-day basis.

*Our fate is determined by how far
we are prepared to push ourselves to
stay alive – the decisions we make to
survive. We must do whatever it takes
to endure and make it through alive.*

BEAR GRYLLS

234

Babysit a friend's child or pet.

*Find happiness in all creatures
small and large, furry or finned.*

UNKNOWN

235

Check out scientist Emoto's
water experiment pictures
online – fascinating.

*My fake plants died because I did
not pretend to water them.*

MITCH HEDBERG

236

Write a love song and
sing it to someone.

*A bird does not sing because it has an
answer. It sings because it has a song.*

CHINESE PROVERB

237

Breathe deeply in through
one nostril while holding
the other closed and then
breathe out through the
other nostril, twenty times.

*Ambition may be defined as the willingness
to receive any number of hits on the nose.*

WILFRED OWEN

238

Take an improv class.

*The only real mistake here is
ignoring the inner voice.*

DEL CLOSE

239

Today, try saying "Yes, I
can" to everything.

*The big question is whether you are going
to say a hearty yes to your adventure.*

JOSEPH CAMPBELL

240

Read Rumi poetry.

*Even death is not to be feared by
one who has lived wisely.*

THE BUDDHA

241

Throw a coin in a fountain or
stream and make a wish.

*Wish on everything. Pink cars are good,
especially old ones. And stars, of course,
first stars and shooting stars. Planes will
do if they are the first light in the sky and
look like stars. Wish in tunnels, holding
your breath and lifting your feet off the
ground. Birthday candles. Baby teeth.*

FRANCESCA LIA BLOCK

242

Wear different coloured
socks on each foot today.

*I'll tell you one thing you can't do: you can't
put your shoes on, then your socks on.*

FLAVOR FLAV

243

Try a meal on the menu today
you normally wouldn't order.

*You will enrich your life immeasurably
if you approach it with a sense of
wonder and discovery, and always
challenge yourself to try new things.*

NATE BERKUS

244

Try greeting everyone today, saying 'hello' in a different language.

'Meow' means 'Woof' in Cat.

GEORGE CARLIN

245

Have you created a detailed business and marketing plan?

Nobody ever wrote down a plan to be broke, fat, lazy or stupid. Those things are what happen when you don't have a plan.

LARRY WINGET

246

Listen to what isn't being said
in daily conversations.

*I've always believed that if you are
precise in your thoughts, it's not the
lines you say that are important — it's
what exists between the lines. What I'm
compelled by most is that transparency
of thought, what is left unspoken.*

VERA FARMIGA

247

When at your local coffee shop,
pay for the coffee of somebody
in the line behind you – pay it
forward and they may then, in turn,
pay for somebody behind them.

A kind gesture can reach a wound
that only compassion can heal.

<small>STEVE MARABOL</small>

248

Let it go. Anger gets stored
and becomes **dis-ease**.

*Holding on to anger is like grasping a hot
coal with the intent of throwing it at someone
else; you are the one who gets burned.*
THE BUDDHA

249

Wear a pair of
rose-coloured glasses and
see your world a little rosier.

*To change ourselves effectively, we first
have to change our perceptions.*
STEPHEN R. COVEY

250

Bend your knees, feet apart, body relaxed and gently bounce for fifteen minutes to help your lymph glands release toxins.

The best way to detoxify is to stop putting toxic things into the body and depend upon its own mechanisms.

ANDREW WEIL

251

Wash a car by hand today
and detail the inside.

*Why can't car washes be giant waterslides
for cars? Speaking of fun, why can't
sex be fun, rather than something you
begrudgingly pay for, like taxes.*

JAROD KINTZ

252

Go kayaking in nature.

*The real voyage of discovery consists
not in seeking new landscapes
but in having new eyes.*

MARCEL PROUST

253

Cut down on your coffee intake.

*My point is, life is about balance.
The good and the bad. The highs
and the lows. The piña and the colada.*

Ellen DeGeneres

254

Try a new food from a different
region of the world.

*We all eat, and it would be a sad
waste of opportunity to eat badly.*

Anna Thomas

255

Go to the symphony.

*A **symphony** must be like the world – it must embrace everything.*

GUSTAV MAHLER

256

Write down the things that stand in the way of your having the career of your dreams – and **burn** it!

Have you ever struggled to find work or love, only to find them after you had given up? This is the paradox of letting go. Let it go, in order to achieve.

UNKNOWN

257

Bake a birthday cake for yourself,
even if it's not your birthday.

*All the world is birthday cake, so
take a piece, but not too much.*

GEORGE HARRISON

258

Take a sniff of pepper and
make yourself sneeze.

An orgasm is just a reflex, like a sneeze.

RUTH WESTHEIMER

259

Get dirty.

If it is the dirty element that gives pleasure to the act of lust, then the dirtier it is, the more pleasurable it is bound to be.

Marquis de Sade

260

Buy a smoothie for a stranger today.

You cannot do a kindness too soon because you never know how soon it will be too late.

Ralph Waldo Emerson

261

Bid on auction items at a
fundraiser of your choice.

*My first car, I got it in an auction at my
temple. It was an '86 Volvo that
I got for 500 bucks, and then wound
up throwing $10,000 into the stereo
system and put TVs in the foot rests.
It was the most ridiculous Volvo you'd
ever seen, but I had never had money
before and I was out of my mind.*

Shia LaBeouf

262

Take a local circus class and walk the tightrope and suspend on silks.

Life is always a tightrope or a feather bed. Give me the tightrope.

EDITH WHARTON

263

Buy a slide-whistle and use it when you manifest success at work.

Your destiny is to fulfil those things on which you focus most intently. So choose to keep your focus on what is truly magnificent, beautiful, uplifting and joyful. Your life is always moving toward something.

RALPH MARSTON

264

Give thanks for the food you
eat and give thanks to the
plants that gave for you.

Man's heart away from nature becomes hard.

STANDING BEAR

265

Ride a bike.
Bicycling is a big part
of the future. It has to be.

There's something wrong
with a society that drives a
car to work out in a gym.

BILL NYE

266

Get a foot massage and pedicure.

*Think of the magic of that foot,
comparatively small, upon which your
whole weight rests. It's a miracle — and
the dance is a celebration of that miracle.*

MARTHA WASHINGTON

267

Sing songs around a bonfire
at a friend's cottage.

*When you do something, you should
burn yourself up completely, like a good
bonfire, leaving no trace of yourself.*

SHUNRYU SUZUKI

268

Never say 'Never'.

I don't think you should ever say, 'This is the last time'. Music isn't like that. You'll be sitting there not wishing to get onto a stage again for maybe two, three, four, five months, or maybe a year, then suddenly you'll wake up and feel like you've got to do it again. It's in the blood, and I never say never.

ROGER DALTREY

269

Tie your shoelaces using a different knot than your usual choice.

I think what it does is it gives me a much broader perspective than the average politician's. You know, having walked in those shoes of being hungry and being homeless. The indignities of not getting health care, or waiting in the public hospital, hoping somebody will care for you. Going to sleep with a toothache because you can't go to the dentist.

RICHARD CARMONA

270

Contact an old friend from your past that you've lost touch with.

Life can be found only in the present moment. The past is gone, the future is not yet here, and if we do not go back to ourselves in the present moment, we cannot be in touch with life.

THICH NHAT HANH

271

In a walking meditation today,
envision shrinking yourself
so small you disappear, then
expand yourself and grow
bigger than the sky.

*I proclaim my blessed ascent from this
binding firmament. My soul soars, unbound,
to unknown seas of the universe.*

SKYE

Go to your local aquarium and
swim with dolphins or sharks.

*Believe in yourself, not only in swimming,
but in life itself. You always have to have fun.
You have to have an open mind. If you're
not enjoying it, don't do it. Life's too short.*

DEBBIE MEYER

273

Remember we are **one** powerful life force, united and bound together.

There is a vitality, a life force, an energy, a quickening that is translated through you into action, and because there is only one of you in all time, this expression is unique. And if you block it, it will never exist through any other medium and will be lost.

Martha Graham

274

Quit a habitual negative habit today.

Avoid destructive thinking. Improper negative thoughts sink people. A ship can sail around the world many, many times, but just let enough water get into the ship and it will sink. Just so with the human mind.

ALFRED A MONTAPERT

275

Give of your vast spirit and
you shall rekindle the earth.

*The place to improve the world is first in
one's own heart and head and hands.*

Robert M. Pirsig

276

What beauty has been revealed
to you lately. Delight in this .

*People are like stained-glass windows. They
sparkle and shine when the sun is out, but
when the darkness sets in, their true beauty
is revealed only if there is a light from within.*

Elisabeth Kubler-Ross

277

Read a great book.

The love of books, the golden key
that opens the enchanted door.

ANDREW LANG

278

Don't be afraid to ask
for what you need.

The squeaky wheel gets the grease.

PROVERB

279

Delegate.

The best executive is the one who has sense enough to pick good men to do what he wants done, and self-restraint enough to keep from meddling with them while they do it.

THEODORE ROOSEVELT

280

Be humble. Humility is the key ingredient to success.

'Thank you' is the best prayer that anyone could say. I say that one a lot. Thank you expresses extreme gratitude, humility, understanding.

ALICE WALKER

281

Cut out the excess. Only use what you absolutely need.

I think frugality drives innovation, just like other constraints do. One of the only ways to get out of a tight box is to invent your way out.

JEFF BEZOS

282

Today, put yourself first.

There is nothing noble about being superior to some other man. The true nobility is in being superior to your previous self.

HINDU PROVERB

283

There is no room for judgement
of any kind. Have an opinion
without judgement.

*If you judge people, you have
no time to love them.*

UNKNOWN

284

Use environmentally
friendly products.

*The most important thing about global
warming is this: it's all of our responsibility
to leave this planet in better shape for the
future generations than we found it.*

MIKE HUCKABEE

285

Write a rave, five-star theatrical
review of your life to date.

*The more you praise and celebrate your
life, the more there is in life to celebrate.*

OPRAH WINFREY

286

Apologize for any bad
action or bad speech.

*I have learned that
sometimes 'sorry' is
not enough. Sometimes
you actually have to change.*

CLAIRE LONDON

287

Never take the same trail
home that you left from
initially. Tread a new path

To whatever wonders unknown await us.
UNKNOWN

288

Pick a bouquet of wild flowers.

*Flowers are the sweetest things God ever
made, and forgot to put a soul into.*
HENRY BEECHER

289

Always go for
'the whole nine yards'.

*(That's an old Scottish saying regarding
yardage used in a top-of-the-line kilt!)*
Anything worth doing is worth doing well.

LORD CHESTERFIELD

290

Walk instead of driving the
few blocks to the store.

*All truly great thoughts are
conceived while walking.*

FRIEDRICH NIETZSCHE

291

Trill your tongue and blow
air through your lips and
then turn it into a whistle.

Whistle while you work.

DISNEY

292

Purpose gives us meaning
and direction and makes
life worth living.

*Your purpose in life is to find your purpose
and give your whole heart and soul to it.*

THE BUDDHA

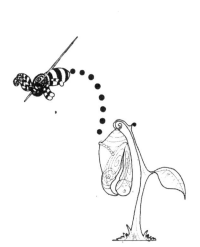

293

Don't live someone else's idea of
what your life should look like.

*If you don't take a chance to live your
life, what can you say at the end if it?*

NAVEEN ANDREWS

294

Think about what gives you
courage during challenging
moments. Build this strength.

*The test of courage on earth is to
bear defeat without losing heart.*

ROBERT GREEN INGERSOLL

295

Use less plastic and reduce
your carbon footprint.

Save the world, it's worth a life or two.

Unknown

296

Skip stones across
the top of a local lake.

Pretty Stones.

Virginia Woolf

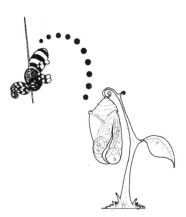

297

Discover your authentic, exciting,
fulfilling and prosperous destiny
by knowing your arrival point.

*The arrival of spring cannot be
painted in one picture.*
DAVID HOCKNEY

298

What makes life worth living?
Are you experiencing it?

*It is only in adventure that some
people succeed in knowing
themselves – in finding themselves.*
ANDRÉ GIDE

299

Keep a daily journal.

Whether you're keeping a journal or writing as a meditation, it's the same thing. What's important is you're having a relationship with your mind.

NATALIE GOLDBERG

300

Tune in to the vast silence within you and receive abundant messages.

Silence is the sleep that nourishes wisdom.
FRANCIS BACON

301

No fear.

There is no fear when you are having fun.
WILL TOMAS

302

Love both your parents
equally – they gave you life, parts
of themselves, and if you disregard
one of them you disregard life.

*I thank God that I am a product of my
parents. They infected me with their
intelligence and their energy for life. I'm
grateful that I know where I come from.*

SHAKIRA

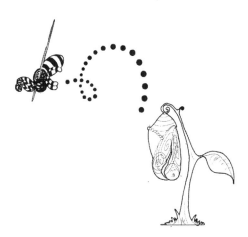

303

Break some personal rules today.

If you obey all the rules, you miss all the fun.

KATHERINE HEPBURN

304

Allow others to help you heal, grow
and conquer your dark moments.

A flower cannot blossom without sunshine.

MAX MULLER

305

Light a fire and re-ignite
your passion, purpose and
intent to live your dreams.

To dream by night is to escape your life.
To dream by day is to make it happen.

STEPHEN RICHARDS

306

Make humility a major
ingredient in your daily life.

Humility is the solid foundation of all virtues.

CONFUCIUS

307

Find your personal centre of gravity
and everyone around you will sense
it and respond favourably to you.

Love is metaphysical gravity.

R. BUCKMINSTER FULLER

308

You are **not** alone.

Look at the sky. We are not alone.
The whole universe is friendly to us
and conspires only to give the best
to those who dream and work.

APJ ABDUL KALAM

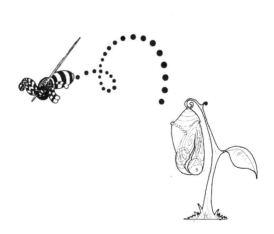

309

Buy the farm!

*Earth is the place where
choice and destiny meet.*

CAROLINE MYSS

310

Tap into your authentic
power, your true strength.

Self-acceptance is pure power.

AMY LEIGH MERCREE

311

You are you-nique. Nothing
in this world has your exact
blueprint – oh wondrous you! –
so don't be afraid to be you.

*You are the only you God made. God
made you and broke the mold.*

Max Lucado

312

Stop striving for goals in the future
and live in the glorious **now**.

It's being here now that's important.
There's no past and there's no future.
Time is a very misleading thing.
All there is ever, is the now.
We can gain experience from the past,
but we can't relive it; and we can hope for
the future, but we don't know if there is one.

GEORGE HARRISON

313

Really get to know yourself and
fall in love with yourself and have
the most amazing relationship.

*When you're different, sometimes you
don't see the millions of people who
accept you for what you are. All you
notice is the person who doesn't.*

JODI PICOULT

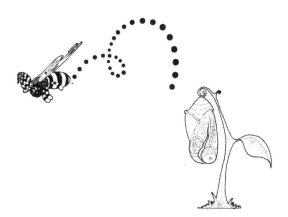

314

Read with one eye closed
and then switch eyes.

*Mind training matters. It is not just a
luxury, or a supplementary vitamin
for the soul. It determines the quality
of every instant of our lives.*

MATTHIEU RICARD

315

Leave your ego at the door.

*When you can abandon your ego
and develop your character you will
be on your way to success in life.*

JOE MEHL

Leave classical music playing
in your home when you are not
there – the plants will thrive
as well as your animals.

*If music is a place, then Jazz is the
city, Folk is the wilderness, Rock is
the road, Classical is a temple.*

VERA NAZARIAN

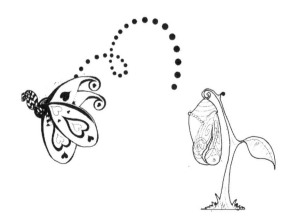

317

Paint some coloured hardboiled eggs and crack the end together with a friend while making a wish. Whoever's shell doesn't crack on the top, gets their wish.

But... well, Reg, tomorrow the sun will come up again, and I'm pretty sure that whatever happens we won't have found Freedom, and there won't be a whole lot of Justice, and I'm damn sure we won't have found Truth. But it's just possible that I might get a hard-boiled egg.

TERRY PRATCHETT

318

Carve a face into a pumpkin and
roast and salt the seeds to munch.

*Only the knife knows what goes
on in the heart of a pumpkin.*

SIMONE SCHWARZ-BART

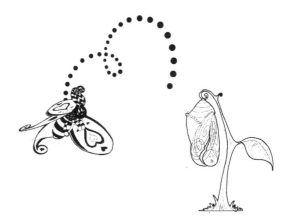

319

Turn off **all** the electricity tonight and eat a picnic outside by candlelight, no hot water. Enjoy the dark and delight in giving Mother Nature a break.

Every time the wind blows I think of her. I wonder if I could generate electricity off my yearning. Maybe a mind wind farm of some kind. Hopefully I could provide enough power for all the lonely people in my bathtub to stay warm.

JAROD KINTZ

320

Wear your shirt backwards or
underpants inside out for good luck.

*In the long run, you make your own luck —
good, bad or indifferent.*

LORETTA LYNN

321

Take yourself to a theatrical
production and clap longer than
you should at the end of the
show and rise to your feet.

*The applause is a celebration not only
of the actors but also of the audience. It
constitutes a shared moment of delight.*

JOHN CHARLES POLANYI

322

Tell a knock-knock joke
that you made up today.

*The most wasted of all days
is one without laughter.*

E. E. CUMMINGS

323

Learn how to say "Hello,
how are you" in sign language.

*But people who think they can project
themselves into deafness are mistaken
because you can't. And I'm not talking
about imagining what a deaf person's
whole life is like. I even mean just
realizing what it is like for an instant.*

RICHARD MASUR

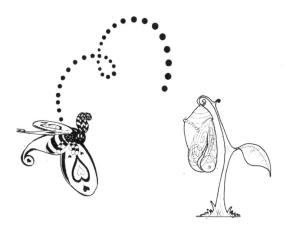

324

Create an equal playing field
and play, not to win, but for
the love of playing the game.

*It's important that athletes can compete
on a level playing field. And youngsters
coming into the sport can know that if they
are working hard and training hard, they'll
see a true reflection of where they stand
and what they can achieve worldwide and
not be swayed by people who are cheating.*

Paula Radcliffe

325

Take the dollar sign out of
the equation today and don't
worry about the cost.

Value is more expensive than price.

Toba Beta

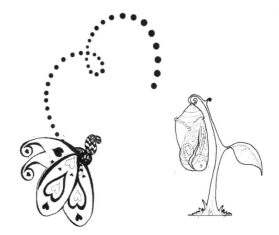

326

Get into a fun debate today.

I love argument, I love debate. I don't expect anyone just to sit there and agree with me, that's not their job.

MARGARET THATCHER

327

Everything dirty comes out in the wash. Do your personal laundry.

An actress once advised me, 'Make sure you do your own laundry — it will keep you honest.'

CATE BLANCHETT

328

Sacrifice something for
someone today.

*It is a far, far better thing that I do than I
have ever done; it is a far, far better rest
that I go to than I have ever known.*

CHARLES DICKENS

329

Love more than you
thought possible.

*If you're going to doubt something,
doubt your own limits.*

Don Ward

330

What eternal, internal mysteries
are begging to be unveiled today?

*Look up at the stars and not down at
your feet. Try to make sense of what
you see, and wonder about what makes
the universe exist. Be curious.*

Stephen Hawking

331

Try using both your left and right brain together today – the logical and the creative.

Any man could, if he were so inclined, be the sculptor of his own brain.

Santiago Ramón y Cajal

332

Be aware of your posture.

Hold your head up high, shoulders back, spine straight. Stand tall A good stance and posture reflect a proper state of mind.

MORIHEI UESHIBA

333

Remember, as delicious as a huge chocolate Easter bunny may appear, it can be hollow on the inside. Don't be fooled by this type of appearance in real life.

Let us be grateful to the mirror for revealing to us our appearance only.

SAMUEL BUTLER

334

Visit that most beautiful place on
earth today – your own heart.

*The best and most beautiful things in the
world cannot be seen or even touched –
they must be felt with the heart.*

HELEN KELLER

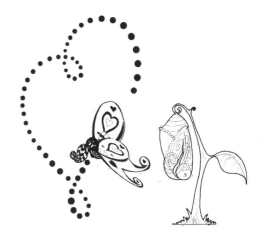

335

Think about impermanence.
Nothing ever remains the same —
we are constantly transforming.

*And when all the wars are over, a
butterfly will still be beautiful.*
RUSKIN BOND

336

Do not disallow your
feelings but allow them to
be expressed more fully.

*Unexpressed emotions will never
die. They are buried alive and will
come forth later in uglier ways.*
SIGMUND FREUD

337

Remain present and accountable
each moment. Don't be asleep
at the wheel and miss **life**.

*It is wrong and immoral to seek to
escape the consequences of one's acts.*

MAHATMA GANDHI

Re-align your mental, physical,
emotional and spiritual
life and become whole.

*Just as your car runs more smoothly
and requires less energy to go faster
and farther when the wheels are in
perfect alignment, you perform better
when your thoughts, feelings, emotions,
goals, and values are in balance.*

BRIAN TRACY

339

We are all caterpillars waiting
to spread our wings.

*And I wonder if the caterpillar at
the threshold of death ever knew
that she would get metamorphosed
into a butterfly that could fly.*

CHIRAG TULSIANI

340

Sign a petition to help
save something.

*Personal transformation can and does have
global effects. As we go, so goes the world,
for the world is us. The revolution that will
save the world is ultimately a personal one.*

MARIANNE WILLIAMSON

341

Pray for someone who
is suffering today.

*We must learn to regard people less in the
light of what they do or omit to do, and
more in the light of what they suffer.*

DIETRICH BONHOEFFER

342

Climb far, your goal the
sky, your aim the stars.

*The will to win, the desire to
succeed, the urge to reach your full
potential – these are the keys that will
unlock the door to personal excellence.*

CONFUCIUS

343

You have specific gifts and personal tools to create an extraordinary life. Recognize these gifts.

You have a unique gift to offer this world. Be true to yourself, be kind to yourself, read and learn about everything that interests you and keep away from people who bring you down. When you treat yourself kindly and respect the uniqueness of those around you, you will be giving this world an amazing gift... You!

STEVE MARABOLI

344

Post your favourite inspirational quote or you tube video on a social media site – share inspiration.

Vulnerability is the birthplace of connection and the path to the feeling of worthiness. If it doesn't feel vulnerable, the sharing is probably not constructive.

BRENE BROWN

345

See the cup half-**full**,
not half-empty.

*We are all in the gutter, but some
of us are looking at the stars.*

OSCAR WILDE

346

Take out an ad in your local
newspaper loving the world.

*Advertisements contain the only truths
to be relied on in a newspaper.*

THOMAS JEFFERSON

347

Put on earphones and listen
to theta brainwave music
before going to bed.

*Music is a higher revelation than
all wisdom and philosophy.*

LUDWIG VAN BEETHOVEN

348

Google the glass pyramid, found at the bottom of the sea in the Bermuda Triangle – Atlantis.

Be open to ideas and thoughts you disagree with. It will unleash a debate in your mind and soul.
JAMES KIRK BISCEGLIA

349

Give a bigger tip than usual.

Unexpected kindness is the most powerful, least costly, and most underrated agent of human change.
BOB KERREY

350

Go for a long brisk walk or run
and breathe in as much oxygen
as your lungs can hold and
then let out a yelp or holler.

*To be human is to keep rattling
the bars of the cage of existence,
hollering, 'What's it for?'*
ROBERT FULGHUM

351

Take food to the food bank today.

We know that a peaceful world cannot long exist, one-third rich and two-thirds hungry.

JIMMY CARTER

352

Look up a free event in your local newspaper that you have never attended and experience something out of the ordinary.

You cannot create experience.
You must undergo it.

ALBERT CAMUS

353

Go line dancing and learn some new steps while letting your hair down and creating a sweat.

The only way to make sense out of change is to plunge into it, move with it, and join the dance.

ALAN WATTS

354

Send your boss a thank you
note and gift for no reason.

Thanks, sir; all the rest is mute.

WILLIAM SHAKESPEARE

355

What kind of hero or heroine would
you be if a movie were made of you?

*Heroes are made by the paths they choose,
not the powers they are graced with.*

BRODI ASHTON

356

Wish on a shooting star
on a clear night.

*I conclude, therefore, that this star is not some
kind of comet or a fiery meteor... but that
it is a star shining in the firmament itself —
one that has never previously been seen, in
any age since the beginning of the world.*

TYCHO BRAHE

357

Be **present**.

*The point of power is always
in the present moment.*
LOUISE L. HAY

358

Go to a photo booth and take pictures of yourself as an undercover agent.

*The photo booth has become Hollywood's
latest trend; celebrities are buying them
for their homes. When the curtain
closes, everybody becomes a superstar.
Their true personality comes out.*
JENNIFER VISHNEVSKY

359

Start a local facebook page and local meet-up group of something that you are interested in and think others would like to share.

The true secret of happiness lies in taking a genuine interest in all the details of daily life.

WILLIAM MORRIS

360

Treat yourself to a triple scoop ice cream, sherbert or frozen yogurt.

Forget art. Put your trust in ice cream.
CHARLES BAXTER

361

Go to karaoke and sing "Hit me with your best shot."

Knock me down, it's all in vain —
I'll get right back on my feet again.
PAT BENATAR

362

See your workplace as a temple and
the words you give as the prayer.

*Work isn't to make money;
you work to justify life.*
MARC CHAGALL

363

Never give up.

Never, never, never give up.

WINSTON CHURCHILL

364

Do what makes you happy.

If you fail, you will be criticized, and if you succeed, you will be criticized. You can't make everyone happy, so you may as well do what makes you happy.

SENORA RAY

365

Kiss: There are no real ends,
only new beginnings.

*Realize that if a door closes, it's because
what was behind it wasn't meant for you.*
MANDY HALE

About Elley-Ray

Elley-Ray Tsipolitis is an actress, director, teacher and humanitarian. She lives in Toronto, Canada and travels to where she is needed. Elley-Ray is an Honorary Doctor of Laws, University of Windsor.

www.Elley-Ray.com

Sources of all the quotations used in *Butterfly Kisses*: Commons.

Acknowledgments

Panagiotis Tsipolitis, John Harris, Anthea Guinness, John McMeekin, Jacki-Dawn McMeekin, Martin Albert, Eric Charbonnea, Kristina Nicoll, Tabitha St Germain, Kevin Bergsma, Edward Roy, Sky Gilbert, David Tomlinson, Clinton Walker, Julie Seip, Stephlynn Robinson, Asti Livingston, Patrick Sweeney, Scott Law, Luke Gordon, Daniel McArthur, Linda Kash, Tilly Kash O'Sullivan, Cameron Elvin, Adrianna Crivici, Grace Gordon, Julia Pileggi, Darryl Hogan, Deb Munro, Sibylle Wagner, Helen Holtham, Kim Hurdon, Dr Tina Pugliese, Julius Cho, and all my students, past and present, who inspire me daily!

SALT RIVER PUBLISHING

Salt River Publishing believes in encouraging artists and publishing professionals to come together and reach their empowered "Yes!"

Salt River was established as a no-profit publisher with the idea of helping writers, translators, poets, graphic artists and photographers bring their work into publishable form.

We provide links to a range of publishing professionals who offer services for anybody with a book in the making.

And we publish books that inspire and encourage, including ones that deepen the understanding of mysticism.

Do you have one?

www.SaltRiverPublishing.com

SALT RIVER BOOKLIST

- *The inner way: a mystic anthology of songpoems, stories, reflections* arranged with translations and notes by Anthea Guinness (SRP, 2013)
- *Stumbling towards enlightenment: a Yoga 101 collection* by Shanan Harrell (SRP, 2014)
- *Teach with Spirit: the teacher's inward journey guide* by Janice Fletcher, EdD (SRP, 2015)
- *Community adventure: the story of Long Dene School* by Sue Smithson (SRP)

Tuppany books
- *Wake up! if you can: mystic sayings of Kabir* with translations and notes by Anthea Guinness (SRP, 2014)
- *Dawn has come: mystic songpoems of Paltu* with translations and notes by Anthea Guinness (SRP, 2014)
- *Coming of age: notes from the front line of aging* by Rosemary Rawson (SRP, 2014)

New Moon books
+ *Butterfly kisses* by Elley-Ray Tsipolitis (SRP, 2015)

Books published independently with Salt River assistance (editing, book design, cover design)
+ *Spiral up! 127 Energizing Options to be your best right now* by Chloe Faith Wordsworth (2014)
+ *Quantum change made easy: breakthroughs in personal transformation, self-healing and achieving the best of who you are* by Chloe Faith Wordsworth (2007)
+ *The fundamentals of Resonance Repatterning*, and eleven other Resonance Repatterning practitioner manuals by Chloe Faith Wordsworth (2007–2015)
+ *Dark bread and dancing: the diaries of Sue Rawson* by Rosemary Rawson(2013)

www.SaltRiverPublishing.com

COLOPHON

Typefaces: Curlz MT (designed by Carl Cross-grove and Steve Matteson), Bernhard Modern (designed by Lucian Bernhard), Adobe Jensen Pro (designed by Nicolas Jensen and Robert Slimbach)

Software: Adobe InDesign

Editing: Salt River Publishing

Book Design and Composition: Carol White of Salt River Publishing (*email:* carol@saltriver publishing.com)

Cover art and flipbook art: Jarrod Elvin www.mick-macks.com

Printer: createspace.com

Printing method: Print-on-Demand (POD) digital printing

Paper: Library quality

Binding: Perfect binding

AUTHORS NEED READERS

If you have enjoyed this Salt River book, please **recommend it** to your friends!

   Authors and artists publish their work because they want to share. **Readers** love new books. We invite **you** to take part in **lifting spirits** and **helping authors** attain their goal. "The right words at the right time can turn a life around…"

+ **Give a copy** to friends – including book groups, study groups and your local library
+ **Write about it online** – emails, blogs, "like it" on social media, a candid review at Amazon

   Thank you from all of us – the writers, artists, editors and designers associated with the no-profit Salt River Publishing company.

www.SaltRiverPublishing.com

READER RESPONSE
TO SALT RIVER BOOKS

"So many problems are spiritual in nature. And healing often involves finding meaning, purpose and spiritual uplift. The right words at the right time can turn a life around. Therapists and practitioners can point the way for clients who are seeking meaning; writers and artists have an opportunity to share in that work. Thank you, Salt River."

Proof